A God Hangs Upside Down

Essential Poets Series 67

Joseph Maviglia

A God
Hangs Upside Down

Guernica
Toronto / New York
1994

© Joseph Maviglia and Guernica Editions Inc., 1994
All rights reserved.

Antonio D'Alfonso, editor,
Guernica Editions Inc.,
P.O. Box 117, Station P, Toronto (Ontario), Canada M5S 2S6
340 Nagel Drive, Cheektowaga, N.Y. 14225-4731, U.S.A.

The publisher gratefully acknowledges the financial support from
The Canada Council and Canadian Heritage (Multiculturalism).

Typesetting by Jean Yves Collette.
Printed in Canada.

Legal Deposit – Second Quarter
National Library of Canada and
Bibliothèque nationale du Québec.

Library of Congress Catalog Card Number: 93-81061

Canadian Cataloguing in Publication Data

Maviglia, Joseph, 1953-
A gods hangs upside down

(Essential poets ; 67)
ISBN 1-55071-014-1

I . Title.   II . Series

PS8576 . A8576G64   1994   C811 ' . 54   C94 - 900214 - 3
PR9199 . 3 . M38G64   1994

Contents

A Nest of Wind

Stone 11
Carlo's Dream 12
The Job Is God 13
New Language 14
In the Still of Night 16
Pomodoro 17
Twenty-One 18
Carlo's First Born 19
Heels Clicking 22
Second Son 23
Accordion Player 24
Mezzogiorno 25
Good Grape 27
The Widow 28
Brancaleone 29
Zampogne 32
Lost Sister 33
Nino's Work 35
Disoccupation 36
I Have No Other Eyes 38
Pescatore di Brancaleone 39
Broken Marriage 40
Spaghetti Westerns 41

The Song a Shovel Makes

Carlo 45
Workman 48

Paolo di Pietro	50
These bastards that I work for	51
Salvatore	52
Portuguese John	54
Unlike Napoleon	55
Job	56
Dust and Gravel	57
We are old	59
Sweat	60
Widower	61
Shutdown	62
I ask him only to move	63
Asphalt	64
Sledgehammer	65
Rain	68
My two sons	69
Paving in Fort Saint John, B.C.	70
Cement and Sun	72
Better Pay: Office Work	73
Ritual	74
There Is a Country	76
A Quiet Place	81
The Song a Shovel Makes	83
On Winning a Juno Award	85
The Fields of Winter	87
Tarantella	90
The Portuguese on College Street	92
The Song Is a Poem	94
Cantatore	96
Columbus	97
Tarantella II	100
College Street	102

Canadian Broadcasting Corporation 105
In this Fiction 107
Man Pulling a Star from His Throat:
    Poem for a Refugee 108

Per mio fratello e le mei sorelle

A Nest of Wind

Who weeps? I not, believe me: on the rivers
race exasperated, flailed by a lash,
the sombre horses, the lightning flashes
of sulphur. I not, my race has knives
that blaze and moons and wounds that burn.

> SALVATORE QUASIMODO
> *The Dead Guitars*

Stone

In a house
somewhere before centuries
a man
I thought might be my father
lifted a stone
under it finding nothing
but his will to toss it into the sea.
And I
not truly of a shape I recognized
turned to mountains I had never seen
laughing as I wrapped
foil from the present age
around a smaller stone
throwing it through light and time
where never caught
a saddened face
recalled hands moving rapidly
without clocks
without machines
wordless
and involved in shaping
what it would never know.

Beside that house I stayed
a womb I could not enter
losing light
for a moment
before the birth of fire.

Carlo's Dream

And there Carlo stood.

A crude Calabrian sun tinting his skin
the colour of light olives.

He stood erect. Knew that though the sun
adored his body
adoration could not feed his children.

So he pushed off on burning feet
sun calling after him.

Leaving the shoreline of his birth
he crawled from mute sea-green
tongue new
           American.

The Job Is God

Carlo has slit the throats of pigs. Holds
a Calabrian bride
made strong by mountain air.

Christ has travelled with him
but there is no sacrament to match
his gathering of wealth.

Pig throats become the new country. Green
and quickly crossed by car.

The job
has always been his worshipped one.
The new land laughing
Carlo's hands reveal a pagan song.

New Language

Carlo needs a family to make his dream come true.
Franco, first born,
brought to Canada at age one,
will go to school and learn the language
that plagues Carlo day and night.

The bosses all speak this language. Its tone,
mixed with the grating of machines,
digging deep in earth where unbuilt highways sleep,
takes the breath of men
who had a language of their own
before it cracked against a deaf Atlantic.

Carlo knows his body can last fifty more years.
Back in Calabria, his father gathered metal
town to town on foot until the age of eighty.
Having come to Canada twenty years ago,
his uncle still digs sewer lines
and brings good money home to a family of four.

Carlo does not want the speech of teachers. Body
will be his pencil. Sons and daughters will use ink.
First, Carlo must learn to shovel. Asphalt
must be handled swiftly,
laid properly before the rakemen's feet.

Carlo sees the faster that he shovels,
the harder it is for the rakemen
and knows he can rake faster if given the chance.
Only days into Carlo's first job, his boss,

impatient with slack rakers,
fires them, and hands the rakes to Carlo
and his boyhood friend, Filippo.

Filippo has raked before. When regulars
called in sick,
Filippo would fill in and do the work of two.
Carlo is happy. Together
they will show the boss the best of their small village.

Carlo and Filippo
turn in the most productive day the boss seen.

He invites them for a drink as the work day ends,
takes them to a tavern
and offers them women for the night.

Filippo has one drink and goes home to his wife.
Carlo stumbles out the tavern door,
arm around a woman who speaks the language well.

In the Still of Night

Awake, Carlo calls back green valleys
olive trees
the salted Mediterranean.

He longs to walk paths worn by Cæsars
a Garibaldi at his side.

Like a bandit deep in silent hills
his heart seeks refuge.

And with every passing heartbeat
one foot off and one foot on new country
he stalks treasure in a sea of strangers.

Pomodoro

From planting until her thumbs are brown
to picking ripe tomatoes, toil
turns Concetta's face to shining sun.

Carlo, home from a hot day of laying asphalt,
tugs her plants up by their roots.

'Don't pull them yet!' she scolds.

Cursing, he continues. Ripping greens from earth
he beats winter to the punch.

Knowing the price of tomatoes in cans
Concetta frowns upon the day
she left a village growing plants into December.

Twenty-One

Concetta's brow tightens
with the thought of playing card games.

'Just one. I'll show you,' Carlo persists.

She turns her card over
exposing
the Queen of Spades.

'You're not supposed to show it!'

'Why not?'

'You need another one at least.'

'What then?'

Impatient, Carlo deals a second card.

'What now?' Concetta questions
holding up an ace.

Carlo's First Born

Carlo never takes Franco to the poolhall.

Before buying his first car,
Carlo visits a relative early Sunday morning,
leaves Franco there,
and meets with fellow workers for an afternoon of cards.

When he finally buys a Ford,
he tells Franco to keep strangers from it,
and explains he'll pick up bread for Sunday dinner.

Locked in a station wagon for five hours
Franco hums songs to himself,
watches as other fathers take their sons into the bakeshop
and come out, pastries in their hands.

At twelve years old, Franco
writes letters in Italian for Carlo
who is still illiterate.

Franco turns sixteen and Carlo
gives him work on a roadcrew, boasting to men
who mark time cards with an *X*
of his son's reading skills.

Sundays, Carlo still goes to the poolhall
while Franco studies books and mows the lawn.

In the time he has to himself, Franco
builds the best ships and warplanes hobby shops sell,
learns Italian history inside out, and puts
his heart into a new guitar.

Though he has helped Carlo pay the rent,
Franco does not ask Carlo for money
when university begins.

Carlo hopes his son will be a teacher
and marry Filippo's daughter after getting his degree.
Franco wants to be a naval engineer. Has no
interest in a girl he knows as loud.

Arguing with Carlo day and night, Franco
finds himself behind halfway through first semester.
Dropping out, he needs money and accepts
Carlo's offer to work roads again.

Franco is among men working with their hands,
but Carlo has stopped boasting.

Franco only writes for himself now.

On the asphalt crew, Carlo starts a fight
with a rival foreman
who criticizes Carlo giving Franco work.

Carlo wants to start his own company.
Franco only wants to play guitar,
and refuses Carlo's demand to return to university.

In winter, Carlo has a kidney stone removed.
Franco leaves the house by noon
and works late hours in a grocery store.

Carlo begins the spring with another company.
Though the pay is good,
Franco will not work for him.

Carlo visits the poolhall less, but when he does
he invites Franco along.

Franco brings his guitar,
and singing a song about a Calabrian brigand,
puts fire in the workmen's hearts.

The workmen want another song.

Carlo leaves the poolhall
and sits behind the wheel of his Ford.

Heels Clicking

I wonder why
they packed their hearts and crossed
a proud Atlantic?

Locked in their memory, a god
hangs upside down
his sweet tongue purpled into foam,
dangling in a cold piazza.

Talk of travel now
fills the air like riled cats:
Concetta saying, 'Can't you sit still?' –
as Carlo stuffs a deck of cards
into his suit-coat pocket.

'I never have!' he answers. 'It's
in my blood to move!'

Magnetic teeth slash at Concetta's eyes.
The burn of rope on twisted toes
returns to haunt her
as Carlo's heels click down the back porch stairs.

Second Son

Carlo fought a war years ago:
has tattoos to prove it.
Girlies jiggle as he showers and sings
'Giovinezza.'

His brother, dead or lost in battle
never saw Canada
and Carlo thinks he'd love it if he did.

'Battalgione di San Marco. We were
tougher than United States Marines.
The pride of Mussolini's seas.'

'Maybe that's why they hung him
by his toes,' I tease. 'Because
like Christ he thought he could walk on water.'

Carlo turns to me: 'You know,
the older you get,
the more of a jackass you become.'

'Giovinezza' (Youth) was a Fascist marching anthem
of World War Two Italy.

Accordion Player

I hear an accordion player in a dream:
blood's music
playing waves in sea voyage.

Every time his monkey
shakes a cup at passing strangers
cups fill with coins
and faces turn friendly as long as
summer turns to fall.

But winter demands warmth for the monkey's fur
and the accordion player
with only two hands asks himself
if coins are worth his monkey's bitter screams.

Mezzogiorno

My feet scratch the ground.

This is at last Calabria
made of familiar dialect
but sons and fathers don't spill wine
toasting to each other's health.

Instead, sons travel north to German factories
while fathers, hands in pockets,
kick the towns worn cobblestone.

Behind me, where a stunted fig tree
holds its twisted arms to unrelenting sun,
old men whisper
that I've come to find my father's town.

A cabby sneers at my Canadian duffle bag,
has eyed me through the afternoon.
Since I stepped off the Reggio bus.

He waits for me to ask if his cab's free.
When I do he doesn't answer
but grabs my bag and throws it in his car.

As we arrive in Carlo's town
the walls of ruins, streaked with red graffiti
lie low against the sea.

'What do you do in Canada?' the cabby asks.
'Write poems,' I say.
'You're in good company,' he laughs.
'Cesare Pavese was detained here by the Fascists.'

It is the one poet whose book
is tucked in my bag
but remains unopened, so I ask,
'Who's Cesare Pavese?'

'If you don't know,' he says,
'you are no poet.'

Good Grape

Wine-maker Genovese picks his grapes
one by one
off sturdy stems,
throws out the overripes.

A daughter with grey husbandless eyes
turns the presswheel, praying
to October sun
for patience with her father's ways.

Autumn after autumn, eager men have come,
been sorted
and set to wander with bouquets
drunk across the hills.

The Widow

In Brancaleone cousin Pino
takes my arm and invites me for a late night walk.
The lights of small mountain towns
satellite us as he
tells of a peasant
murdered for stealing a goat.

The man's widow works the pastures,
walks to a well at dawn
knowing neighbours' eyes
watch from behind.

Each day, ahead of her,
she sees broken shacks
isolated from the overlord's green land.

The goat wanders freely,
raises its simple horned head
and chews crisp, ripened blades.

At its bleat for water,
the widow grinds her jagged teeth.

Brancaleone

Ce-sa-re Pa-ve-se
the name comes to me in syllables
in syllables
in a language I've inherited
only part of.

U Calabrisi, Calabrian, I
mangle I've been told. This
has kept me close to silent
since I've arrived.

I walk meadows in December
relieving my hands from the pick,
the shovel, the sledgehammer
I have begun to use back home.

Cesare,
you gave the field workers names,
the town woman love,
and poetry a place to come from.

What makes me find a ruin in the wind
and read and reread your book of labour
and love?

Lavorare Stanca. Back home
they call it *Hard Labour*
but it's not the work of hands
compelling me to read on.
It's the fatigue of the sun
so tired

and unable to move the souls of peasants
inheriting land
once ruled by Spaniards, Greeks and Moors.

What is to inherit? Silence?
Peace?
Nostalgia?
The beauty of the summer months?
Truth?

For you
truth was the liberty of words.
The sad eyes of old men
walking these hillsides without women.
For me
truth is someone never met
a voice
almost at times inside me,
never cautious enough in youth
awaiting age
where your words have their light
and do not suffer of my need.

In this town
mules bray against the rooster's rise.
I have no voice
but have the eyes of these field workers.

I'm told my line has
hoed and dug and swung and built
and that kind of living carries pain
as it grows through generations,
after years and years of tired travel.

Cesare, the *Reggitani* live a poetry
unwritten but the song
coming from the fishermen
lives by the luck and tenacity of memory.

Have you found liberty? Dead?
I do not weep.
The tear pooling in my eye
remembers nothing
like the swordfish
always returning for the bait
and the song that feeds
first the flesh
then the silence of the sea.

U Calabrisi is not Italian.
This much I know
and the syllables of absurdity,
my peasant's eyes
are all that I can speak with.

Zampogne

No one starves in this town. Pigs
fattened through summer hang
slaughtered, ready for the evening.

The village *carabinieri*
have closed the jail to join their wives
for the *Night of the Befana,*
a spirit worshipped for the gifts
she brings to poor.

The Germans too have come,
leaving tanned Mercedes' on the outskirts,
the vandals in the pool rooms
too keen to let good business pass them by.

A young boy throws stones at a clown
who leaps onto a bench and blows a shepherd's horn,
while two others
aim their bagpipes towards the sea.

From windows gun shots blast. Announced,
the good saint never comes,
but no mouth goes unfed
because the children take their clowning seriously,
and the vandals wait for the sound of pipes
that tell where cars are parked.

Lost Sister

Since arriving, I've visited
family on Concetta's side, and on Carlo's.

They tell me my godfather has come,
his season's bricklaying done back home.

Last time we met was ten scaffolds up, in Canada,
where he expected me to wash down bricks
with one plank under foot.
I told him he was crazy then
and don't need to repeat it to him now.

But on my last day here
the sea moves calm
and Carlo's brother, Giulio,
sits drunk while my aunt lies in hospital,
having broken her leg as she fell
cleaning stairs.

'How does your father like Canada?'

'Fine. He's working hard.'

'Is he caring for your mother?'

'Yes, but she's alone most of the time.'

Looking up, I see him nodding off.

I go to the stairs where my aunt fell
and climb to an empty room. On a dresser
sits a photograph of a younger Giulio
smiling, and a young girl at his side.

I flip the frame over in my hands.
From the little Calabrian I know, I read:
Maria, the day before she drowned. 1933.

Descending the stairs, I wake Giulio
and walk him to the beach. Foam
running at our feet,
he hurls his empty bottle at the sea.

Nino's Work

Nino has sheared sheep
for thirty years: packed
and carried wool
to lower towns by mule.

This spring
a fabrics factory from Reggio
plans new service
offering synthetics at cut prices.

Nino says, 'My customers – they know
wool is wool.
Besides, my mules know these roads.'

Outside,
beyond the braying stables
truck tires rattle past.

Disoccupation

You open your eye to the bandit's
wind –
Salvatore Giuliano out of the mist
peels a piece of fruit with his knife.

These are the hills of sleep. Americans
and their Second World War graves,
Lucky Luciano and his messages
back home from American jail.

Nothing runs through your blood
as the cats scratch the grass
passing the entrance to a ruin.

Here you can hide. Wait for
the whistle of the young boys
that the *Americani* have arrived.

And the earth no longer hoed
lets the wind take what it wants.
No point in resistance now –
after invasions
nothing good remains. Now

nobody is arriving or expected –
here you can hide.

If you cannot find a tree
to tuck your knife behind
no need to worry. The wind
will scatter you to the sea below.
Here you can hide.

And the brothers and the sisters
not taken by the cross-Atlantic dream
wait at a broken fountain
never good at luck or winning
disoccupied as the fields they walk
with hungry mules
no vision
no new country to escape to
no idea of change
except the wind turning to rain.

Here you can hide. Here
you can peel a piece of fruit.
No one
is coming any more. No one
will be taken away
not bandits
not women and not the sea.

I Have No Other Eyes

I do not jump at the chance
Pino gives me to shoot
a shotgun into a New Year.

Our recognition ends here.
As I stand above him by a foot
he sees me as intruder, uncelebrating.

The gun against my shoulder
is powerless. That my finger
could end a life
or knock a star out of the heavens
stiffens my arm.

Grabbing the gun back
Pino tries to show me the way.
I grab it back.

His eyes expand.
I turn the rifle skyward.

Somewhere a bird
with ears like mine
goes deaf in flight
and thanks his feathers
I have no other eyes.

Pescatore di Brancaleone

There was a war in Carlo's small hometown.
Houses scarred
like faces of the village men
who ride the sea in the afternoon.

Most of the men (the town has few)
rest on the shore. Backs to upturned
rowboats, they carve
paddles for those who have not lost
strength to modern ships.

From the shore they eye the long grey movements,
and the fish, when caught are not for sale,
the men who catch
too proud of nets hand-woven by the shoremen.

As sea line meets dusk,
a fire of wood from worn boats,
conjures up old stories of the day
American planes cracked every wall and window.

And the scent of fish smoke
gives these men
a nest of wind to sleep on,
raising them before the sun
and lulling of the ships upon their waves.

Broken Marriage

Uncle Mimmo's *carabinieri* jaw
shifts
the hazy Milanese air
circling his face.

'The might of Mussolini. We were young –
a *nation* as a family! The true
sense of the word.'

Minutes later beneath Il Duomo's
stained-glass light
he lowers his head and lets
aging knees
squeeze teardrops from his eyes.

By end of day,
on the other side of town
cousins half way through dinner
do not rise to greet us
as my aunt sets out
two extra plates.

Spaghetti Westerns

Remember those old Westerns
shot in Italy?
Highnoons and sunsets with the hero
letting desert wind
flick ashes of his chewed cigar?

The good part was the ending,
the bad, the beginning
and the ugly, your pockets
outdrawn of their money.

You knew the star. Gaunt cheeks,
eyes squinting
on a dusty trail.

It was America to twelve-year-old
Italian boys,
believing for a moment
that America was good
as we believe it must have been
at some point in its past.

The Song
a Shovel Makes

No poet would be there to intone meter of soul's sentence to stone, no artist upon scaffold to paint the vinegary sweat of Christian in correspondence with red brick and grey mortar, no composer attuned to the screaming movement of Job and voiceless cry in overalls.

Pietro di Donato
Christ in Concrete

Carlo

What will they all write
these sons
these daughters who marry
and leave me
here with myself?

If I could write I would tell them
they should never have been born
but they were
and this much we
share

that we came from nowhere
and struggle a lifetime of reason
to say it was somewhere we remember.

Who makes the bed in the morning?
My wife. Why shouldn't she?
Who sleeps in it?

It has gone on so long
and all the tits and ass that come to this
head of mine
have made the mornings
full of sun
full of sadness.

Or should I say
misery?

*If I could write
I'd tell them
that when they leave there will be
nothing they will meet with
that allows them to forget me.*

*If I could write I'd write
not poems
or recollections
but answers to their questions.*

*And if they should ask
why I beat my next door neighbour
for setting his grade so high
water floods my yard
I'd write:*
I hit him hard that day
that day
I hit him hard
because the moon the night before
pulled tides
over a peaceful world.

I'd write that if I could write.

*It would be better if when I did
no one questioned
what I had to say.*

*This whole business of being someone
with something to say
is a way of being
sure not to do much more than
tire a world*

already
tired.
And when he said
that morning
when he said
that stupid son of mine
said,
'Poetry makes nothing happen,'
who is he
to spend his life
turning up the dirt and chasing stars
just to leave every
talk with me
with something stupid
said and written by an old English fool.

If I could write
I would have said:
Poetry is a way of making
sure nobody forgets.

If I were him
I would remember that
if I could write
I'm sure he would remember.

I hit him
that day
hard.
A peaceful world
was pulled by tides because
the moon...

Workman

Today's the last day before the long weekend.
It's after lunch and the sun's
high and strong.
My afternoon's work waits on me.

I must shovel mounds of clay
from around a rotting sewer line,
make room for new pipe going in
first thing next week.

Sand and stone of morning's patchwork
were easier to move
but this clay, it makes me sweat.
I learn to use the energy I build up at lunchtime.
I eat to work I tell myself.
I came to work today.

The afternoon crawls in the hot August sun.
Weight of clay makes my body tight,
each shovelful I move brings greater strength.
My breathing finds its rhythm.

The site boss walks to where I stand,
tells me we are running behind:
'That pipe's gotta be cleared for Tuesday.
It's five o'clock now. Could you stay
a little longer tonight?'

I have nothing special to go home to.
It's just as good I put money in my pocket as go
home to Carlo's weekend chores of cutting wood,
and trimming hedges.

I've had long weekends before.
The pipe's gotta be cleared. That's
all that matters now.

I shovel clay. Make way for new pipe
coming first thing next week.

Paolo di Pietro

Age forty, Rosetta shudders as she
gives birth.
A frail baby girl, husband Paolo
holds her with hands
that have laid a millions bricks.

Last week on thirty-feet-high scaffolds
Paolo trowelled mortar evenly
preached
Jehovah's word to fellow workers.

Home days later,
the infant dies
and Paolo bites his wind parched lips.

These bastards that I work for
every day
day in day out
these bastards make
nothing for me but misery.

There I am. Each day
another animal.
That's all I am. These
bastards
I build my ass off for.
These fools I make highways
and roads for have failed me.

And when I am told
when they tell me
when they say
without a hint of pain
they say
you cannot own a company
because you have no education
isn't it me
I hate the most
or the silly face of God
who laughs and says I've failed
myself?

So much for what I fear. A family
a car
maybe I own enough already
but it's what others have
God is laughing at me for.

Salvatore

Sal never calls it toil or labour.
Each day he swings his pick
hard into earth,
moving heavy chunks with a laugh.

When we break for lunch,
he's the one slapping his thigh,
whistling at the girls,
and telling the best jokes.

With a long thin nose and yellow teeth,
Sal has little choice in looks
but as lunch ends
he's first to set his muscles into motion.

'Ciucciu bellu di stu cori...', his sweet
donkey song,
cuts the thick air of the job site, swings
his body up and down,
making every move seem simple.

Persuaded by his casual approach,
I try a song myself and put my back out
taking concrete slabs off a truck.

That night, Sal visits me at home. Smiling,
he shakes his head from side to side, and says,
'You gotta learn to use you muscles right.'

Back at work two weeks later,
Sal stands by.
Making sure I use my legs when lifting,
he moves away and grins, '*Ciucciu bellu.*'

'*Ciucciu bellu di stu cori...*' translates from a Calabrian folk song as 'Beautiful donkey of my heart...'

Portuguese John

Portuguese John's blue eyes
haven't seen
Azorian shores in years.

When he talks,
the topic's fish
and salted sea.

Other times he's silent
like at lunch break.
Silent as he skins
with one long twirl

an apple underneath
a shady maple.
Skins it
with a six-inch blade.

Unlike Napoleon

Five-foot-two Remo has it rough
getting men to follow
simple orders.

He claps his hands, screaming,
'*Avanti!* Cement is coming!'

We don't budge, but joke about
his reddening doll-face nose.

'Who is the boss here?' he challenges.
'Me or you?'

'We are!' we answer,
as he throws his clean white hardhat
to the ground.

Job

During break
Sam speaks of the good
the company does.

'In five years
I retire back to Italy.'

The crane man teases because
Sam talks broken English.
'Danny, you funny man!'

With break over
Sam goes down the trench
to fit the next pipe
and all the
laughter of a moment past
is silenced

as the trench
wall
swallows
Sammy's
bones.

Dust and Gravel

For Pietro di Donato

Christ in all his forgiveness
does not know the taste of dust.

His gold
his purpled robes his saints

know nothing of the dust against
six men in battle against time
against the needs of company owner
against the threat of being left at home
if you refuse to pull your weight.

Christ, Pietro,
did not hear the scream
of Geremio whose genitals were impaled
on the building's girder rods.

Christ heard that scream no more
than he hears the scream of lungs
bursting over the years of fumes
dust and diesel.

Gravel in all its innocence
three-quarter round or finer
is a colourless grey needed for a highway.
Dust can be what we've been told
we return to.

But, Pietro, I see the men around me
age
I fear my age itself

I do not know the wind in me
how much longer it can last
and whether it will escape in time
the rakes
the constant swing of hammers
picks and rage.

Christ never answered Geremio
and he answers no one here
not Francesco
who gave up his rural past
and still curses the day he left
not young Benito
and the cocaine he needs to
make it through another wasted day
not Sam
crippled and dead under clay and earth.

And João from Lisbon
claims the Calabrians stole
Saint Anthony from the Portuguese.
This he says as he damns
the boss and each Calabrian foreman
in his sights.

This he says
and prays to God from Sunday until
Monday morning
at five a.m.
two hours to prepare
have coffee and kiss his kids
his wife
before Christ arrives and hell begins.

*We are old
we who have taught our sons
endurance
in the face of mistrust
uneven reason
and pride.
We are old.*

*And no will cry
as loud as our women
the day that we die
cry our daughters and sons.*

*We are old.
Like a stone that remembers
how it struggled adrift
one moment noted by ripples
the next by gulping waves
we are old.*

*And birth
as it scurries behind us
still waits ahead*

*with the face of a country
where
years are whispered
into the deaf circle of memory.*

*We are old
we who cannot read.
We who know only to sing.*

Sweat

Filippo's body tilts earthward. Age
sixty-five
and anchored by a shovel,
he has not changed since the day he came.

There have been those
who have made a pass at greater things,
but even Leonardo's want for wings left sweat
on his stern brow.

Filippo's toil is simple.
A shovel full of American dirt
severed from Calabrian soil.

He remembers the day he swam and splashed at waves,
then sat to stare at tankers
bound for a foreign land,
letting the sun soak through his olive skin.

That day long passed. His last
day on the job, he leans
and digs,
feet firmly planted,
sun pulling at his glands.

Widower

For Filippo and Giuseppina

I am an old man dreaming.
Her skin
smooth like ripened plums
is lit by candle flames.

The table set
we talk as though
we had just begun a life
we never knew.

My muscles flex:
their day's work well behind,
only her moist brown hands can tame
my need to move.

The plate before me shines,
grows wider
as my eyes reach then collapse
into an empty dish.

Bare light-bulb overhead is dim,
her body trapped
in cancered skin tells me
I am dreaming.

Shutdown

Cranes are still today.
Strike placards
lull the eyes of men
whose muscles itch in idle air.

Four weeks ago, we had good news:
a project meant to last eight months.

Scraping clay from his rolled-down shirtsleeves,
Remo says, 'The union makes the rules.'

'And what are we to do?' I ask.
'Stand silent like machines.'

I ask him only to move
move the car
so we can pave the road
for him
his kind.

I have worked in this country
this country
and these rich Pakistani
that I make the road for

do they care? Do they
see my calloused hand
my spine of steel?
Do they?

When we
we Italians
more Calabrians than Italians
first came to this country
we were the black ones

we were the ones looked down on
so do not wait for me
do not wait
when I see the way this country's going
do not wait for
me to say
they deserve better. Maybe they do
but what would it matter
if you heard it from me?

What would it matter?

Asphalt

Wind blows the taste of diesel into my mouth.
Work brings out the body muscles.

Derek
a black belt studying law
begins his first day talking
going on about Walter Rodney
and the failure of a people to protect
good politicians.

Boss Remo doesn't care
Derek's from Guyana. Doesn't
see any need for political talk
taking up the morning.

Derek learns this at night.
When Remo drives him home.

When boss Remo drives him home
he has Derek cut his lawn
then the Super's
the company owner's
his whore's
the machine operator's
the engineer's
because to Remo and his friends
Derek's first black
second a body
that protects them from their waste.

Sledgehammer

For the last time I have brought
this hammer down. Down on
concrete sidewalk needing repair.
And, after millions of swings,
labour at best
has always been mind and groin.

Mind enters before every swing
but never stays long. You
beat the dust from in front of your face,
you laugh at the next man who has
hit his foot.
This is a way of living.

My blood is not his blood
and never will be. He is saying
that when I do not sustain myself
through this labour
he will pick up after me,
but not for me.
He is saying he wants me dead,
and I am bound to die, but not this way.

I have brought this hammer down.
I could sing of John Henry
but he is not from the land of my father.

But there is a motion I remember
one man showing.
Like a donkey kicking
his sledge lasted forty years
until his back became
a cracking coil of rusted steel.

When metal meets rock
you either win or die.
The in-between is your blistered
hand. A gash on your shin,
a yell from bossman that the work needs doing.

This is the best romance
has to show for itself: Sampson
became part of the ruins,
the temple his labour.

You die fifteen hours a day
or eight or six or one.

What you have to believe in is your living.
Get over it.
The sun is setting on a tired tool.
Laid down, it wants that old man's motion.

But all you bosses that I've worked for,
understand this.

For all the blood and sweat
exchanged for coins,
remember this.

If you break open the coins
you will see the blood of the worker.
Look further
and you will see
the footprints
made on the beds of sand below your sidewalks.
Made by each one of us.

Some day
a million donkey's hooves
will kick out,
busting concrete,
your eyes
never
quick enough.

Rain

There is nothing asphalt
foremen
hate
asphalt itself
its oil and stone
hates
more than rain

nothing
four hundred degree
asphalt
at fifty dollars a ton
for a twenty-ton load
asphalt hates
as much as rain

nothing six tired bodies
would rather do
as November lays the trees bare
than help their women
shop
take care of a leaky roof
get up to espresso
instead of asphalt

in a bad mood
foremen much the same
and the threat of the next day
being twice as hard
to make up for a day lost
like November rain.

My two sons
Franco
and the poet
one means the future
the other
a fool to language.

The future
has no need for weakness.
No need
for intelligence without action.
If you cannot use your hands
I tell him
then to use his brains. But
he does not. He wallows
and waits
too much his mother's son
too kind
and lacking hunger.

The other
the poet
him I do not think of
in the same way. Him
I think of
as he is
free
as I might have been
had my older brother not died.

Nothing
guides my hands but fate.
And fate it seems
plays a waiting game.

Paving in Fort Saint John, B.C.

Word was there was work
not far from trees
mountains and away from
the same old thing each day

no more dialect wars
between Calabrians and Friulani
just me
somewhere new

so the work started up.
I got to shovel next to cowboys
not really cowboys
in the rope and horse sense

but cowboys when it came to
riding trucks
hauling asphalt
building roads

and for them
because the last one got drunk

I was there Indian
quiet
watching them when I got ahead
waiting for them to catch up

I was there Indian
what else could a Greek –
Spanish –
Moroccan-looking person
be

but a redskin to cowboys
blonde
and shooting ducks at lunch

that's right
shooting ducks at lunch
catching none

driving those old trucks
like they were *Monsterama* stuff
just ghosts to me

and the day the asphalt spreader
broke down from their abuse

the day they called for
a union operator from Vancouver

and his name Stefano
here from Rome fifteen years

good English
and me talking to him in Italian

and the cowboys
saying:

'You Italian?
We thought you wuz an Indian.

Well step right up and have a drink –'

'Well thanks but no thanks all you partners.'
My olive skin now rage red
for the last man they had ruined.

Cement and Sun

My back
tight like the stretch
of an overwound string

explodes
and twists.

The shovel
I have pulled and pushed
the dull grey weight of cement with
stands
stuck, cement drying –
me on the ground.

This is the hardest
friendship.
No one but
the last man who had his spine
cracked by a manhole cover
slipping out of a backhoe's
inattentive hold
knows
once a back goes
it is never the same.

And the rhythm that was mine
the song of a body sunned
given over to labour's symphony
is unheard
under the traffic and machines
of bloated industry
roaring to a hostile sun.

Better Pay: Office Work

'Did you hear the one about Mussolini
and the underwear in North Africa?'
Al asks, trying to get a laugh
from a mundane phone room.

'Hey, I'm going to lunch.
Tell me later,' I answer
sure to get him off my back.

'No. Wait. It's short,' he smiles
as he's been doing for days
since he's found a *wop* to work his phones.

'Anyways, Mussolini says to his troops,
"I gotta soma gooda news, ana soma bad.
Evereebody getsada changa undaweah.
T'ing eese, you changa widda him,
ana you changa widda him ana..."'

'Great stuff Al,' I say,
hoping its his last.
Not for Mussolini's sake but for his own.
Because I'd rather work with men
constructing roads
than making like I'm busy on the phone.

Besides, the pay is better
and the outdoors
keep my underwear light and fresh.

Ritual

Back in '59 Carlo gave Franco and me fifty cents
each to go see *Ben Hur*. We ate popcorn
until our bellies ached, but stayed
long into the afternoon seeing it a second time.

Franco and me once worked together.
On roadcrews in summer
we sang songs, moved earth with picks and shovels,
learning how to use our hands.

But Franco and me no longer work side by side.
When he calls
to see the film years later, the print is faded
and I say I'm glad
Ben never raced down any roads we built.

But Franco can't let go.
He believes roads breed heroes,
and I, that Carlo never said
to watch for Caesars
rising to obliterate a freedom fighter's rage.

Franco's latest plan is to honour family.
Put gondolas in a Canadian city, though
gondolas suggest Marco Polo
more than peasants hoeing fields, the likely
truth of our lineage.

Franco's traced our name back to Madrid,
and claims our ancestors
backed Columbus in his New World journeys.

But I try to get beyond his talk heroes
and speak about a man
who has not lived up to his dreams.

I remind him as he once told me
that when Carlo left Calabria,
he had no backing. Had to admit
a loss of heritage
because the world ahead needed filling in.
I say no emperor greeted Carlo at Halifax Harbour,
wife expecting, fellow travellers in used clothes.

Still, Franco won't let go. Be it
the outlaw Giuliano
liberating peasants from Mafia,
or Michelangelo cursing Christ and His high ceiling,
Franco needs a greater man in Carlo's place.
A man who will walk the memories
of neighbourhood streets and say
the family fighting wasn't worthless.

I can't tell him this. But when
he cries,
his thoughts of Carlo leave him dumb,
lingering with an inherited accent,
chariots and gondolas aside.

There Is a Country

I

There is a country where a man slaps his daughter.
The country of Saveria's heart
where noodles are uneaten
and thrown behind a dowry trunk.
A room in that country
Saveria runs to and cries herself to sleep in.

In Carlo's country
the echo of his slap lingers.
This is where Saveria returns
twenty years later without ally,
fighting hard to change what she remembers.
Where Concetta bore five children to a man
who spends his life building roads for God's America
and has a heart attack.

In Carlo's country a uniform hangs in a closet
waiting to be worn in parade
to celebrate Italy's Second World War fighting men.
Carlo and other men
who have found America since that war
have many daughters.

Saveria has no uniform but remembers
Concetta's tears when Carlo
brought his body home
wearing the perfumes of American women.

In Carlo's country Saveria at nineteen and courting
sees Carlo's hand
slap a young Italian man
who kisses her before he moves her to his home.
The young man leaves America. His love for soccer,
his excuse to leave Saveria.

Another man plays football.
In Carlo's country
American sport relieves the tension of days
locked into asphalt, dust and stone.
In Carlo's country this football player
takes Saveria
moving her across the cities of a new land,
sharing with her a dog,
and giving her nights free to walk alone with it
while he tosses talk and flattery
to barmaids and his mates.

In Carlo's country
Concetta longs for her daughter's company.
Though she is proud of Carlo's fine look in uniform,
her photograph collection has been altered.
When she reaches for her album of Saveria's wedding,
the refection of her eyes on the plastic coating
wears the ghost of a young Italian soccer man. Wears
the fright of photographs consciously misplaced.

Having fought his war for a nation,
Carlo outlives a heart attack with ease.
Having lost a ring
in proposing marriage and not marrying,
a young Italian man returns to his homeland with ease.

Having put his mind to business
and less to sport,
Saveria's husband waits on word from her with ease.

In the country of her heart,
men in uniforms have put up walls,
and leave her thinking of Concetta's dress at funerals.

II

In Carlo's country
a second daughter, Tina, slams doors.
Carlo does not like Tina's man. He has
no old country hands. He
is not unlike the American bosses
Carlo has fought hard to please.

But were this man of Tina's rich,
or some athlete with an American name,
Carlo would bargain,
but Carlo's need to please
goes only as far as it benefits him.

Tina does not bargain well.
The doors slammed stay shut
opening only when she meets strangers
who don't ask questions of her problems.
Like Saveria
she returns to speak to Carlo
but his heart attack returns them to a quiet space.

In Carlo's country
his uniform brings him fresh memory.
The battle with the bosses and women
are alike to him.
But for shovel, pick and rake,
he builds his love as he builds roadways.
When building love, his memory
(a tool to move his heart),
brings back his mother's death,
and the silent block of stone his tears flowed through.

In this country
Carlo does not parade his uniform.
This is where
love wails across the sea, plants itself in a man,
and as in a dream
brings his daughters running from their rooms
for a father's kiss
after a day of labour beats him.

In this dream
(never any further than his memory),
Carlo hopes his daughters and his wife
know his heart is knocking. In this dream

Carlo has retired
and his uniform is pressed. In this dream
Concetta and her daughters
spin above his head
and curse the day that he was born.
In this dream
the curse for him is his redemption.

Carlo's country has a third daughter, Angelina.
She cries, thinking Carlo and Concetta will not know
a child she may bear some day.

To her, family is like learning from a history book.
Because of her young years,
she creates a world ahead her sisters envy.

A country where she will not cry a lifetime.

A Quiet Place

With her children gone, Concetta
spends her days still
waiting for Carlo to come home.

He needs her more than those many years ago,
the day he journeyed up a hillside
and proposed to an aging man
care for his second daughter.

Concetta still roasts peppers for the winter,
does her wash in the bathtub
never using the electric washer
Carlo bought to keep the water bill from going up.

In the living room, plants grow.
On the fireplace mantle,
a picture of Concetta at her mother's grave
is dusted every week,
a plastic flower by its side.

She sits here for long rests.
Between her summer garden and cooking,
game shows on T.V.
her company for hour after hour.

When they were younger, she told her daughters
the greatest gift
a woman could give a man was her loyalty.

This gift she gave to Carlo,
and time knits wrinkles on her hands
as she dreams of the small town where she grew,
her own mother's hands,
the starlight Carlo promised,
and the sighs of hope
she breathes throughout the night.

The Song a Shovel Makes

It is not unlike
the bleeding of a palm too young
to stand with aging men

not unlike
your wrists swollen over ditches
blood pounding before the beat of jackhammers
before the morning deafens
and the afternoon swells
beads of sweat out of your heart.

The song a shovel makes
knows the years gone by
is a boat from Reggio
Messina
Cosenza and Catanzaro

is a song of armour against
the death of rural harvests
the death of parents left in villages
brothers lost in war
mothers in endless black
and the cold wind of arrival.

The song a shovel makes
is the colour of red peppers
ripe tomatoes
and the laughter of the young.

The shovels of a thousand men
know high unemployment
when snow covers the earth.

The song a shovel makes
beats children
when the boss wants greater rhythm.
This is a song
a shovel wished it did not know.

There was a man from Reggio
who did not know his shovel sang.

Day into evening
he dug and tucked in memory
the ditches   roads   bridges.
But his shovel did not answer
when he called
so he looked to gardens for rhythm's
pulse   looked to silence
and it kept him singing.

Shovels can move mountains
with blood running the hands that hold them.
And a mountain
can cry through time
empty of its iron and gold.

This is one song the shovel makes.
No shovel can replace a mountain.
A man can be replaced
his shovel cannot
his song almost never
if his shovel is to sing.

On Winning a Juno Award

Studio klieg lights sharp
my eyes squinting
a crowd of third generation
Italiani
propped up by the producer
cheer at my appearance.

My song
about the lost language
between
a father
and his son
and the hurting dream of toil
swims out of place.

I do not know if they understand
understand
that the song I sing
turns in a generation
and will disappear in a year
dead after it's been rewarded.

...and the land that you grew in
you've never outgrown.
I sing
imagining my father's unsaid words
mine sung now to him.

*...the sun's turned its back
on the moon...*
and thirty seconds to go
*dwells in a country where winter
bites hard
frosts up the windows
and covers the yards...*
five seconds
and the butcher is opened on Monday.
and the song ends.

And the applause rises
as the camera cuts to a raffle
for videos and Francis Ford Coppola
t-shirts
and somewhere this make sense
to someone watching T.V. out there
or maybe my mother
or the mothers of others'
who know a man's dreams don't
always work out
and his son remembers the pain
and that the pain is empty
not enough
so he writes a song
no one will sing but him
no one will hear
except the tears in an old man's blood.

But here I am free
a builder of words
that wash out my soul like the rain
on a road that falls gently behind me
a guitar raised to the sun.

The Fields of Winter

In a gesture of blood both old and new
mine is a heart
composed when passion deep in Ionian seas
surfaced on the shores of Winter.

My amphibious eyes
moved along the sidewalks of industry.
Side to side
life was ahead of me.

Held in a room of crucifixes
I was anointed without choice
with a Catholic shield adorned
my pagan root almost removed.

I was taken to the House of Christ
intoxicated with delirious words
made to wear robes of black and white
and blessed by patriarchs and men of God.

I was left to nights of beasts
raging over my half-closed eyelids
and expected to find peace.

But the Sun and Moon put tools in my hands.
A shovel made of tempered ore
and a pick to open the hostile earth.

From the earth arose great structures
cracking sky and blocking light
while night's beasts cavorted in my blood
to the sound of mules crushing mules.

One night I awoke alone.

I ran to a field
filled with chickens squawking at an axe.
The axe danced without memory.
The blood of slaughter stained my hands.

And the beasts of night ended. No more
was I to hear song from a tree.
No more was I to crawl back to the sea. My body
supple with the strain of toil
rested nowhere and a second Winter had begun.

Fields of grass became black roads.
Structures grew to higher clouds.
My shovel raged and the jewels of labour
housed and comforted against the cold.

And another tool was brought to me.
A brother made of steel.
The clouds could not be seen.
Light no longer existed.
Opened earth cried with each blow.

Breathless I reached for my brother's hand.
Winter grew as he abandoned me.
I cursed the God who had sent him to my side.
I turned my pick and shovel towards my chest
releasing root into the frozen trees.

And Winter came no more. New brothers
climbed out of the sea
with sisters made of wind and seed.
And the sisters laughed with ease
as the Sun and Moon returned.

Light brought the structures tumbling down.
The opened sky washed over a wounded earth.
Sun gave birth again to fire.

No longer alone
I took my shovel and from it formed a mold.
Steel from my first brother's soul
was poured and new shovels held in every hand.
Moon swayed us in her arms of song.

At times I felt the power of my eyes
raise dead trees across pale fields.
Other times wind caressed my breast
and for my sight
my brothers chose to make me a king.

One found the shield
I had cast off long ago and from it
shaped a wreath of gold.
Refusing it I swung my shovel to the sky.
Sweat spilled to the arid soil.

And in this time
after the death of a Catholic God
before the death of Sun and Moon
great cities grew
and shadows found the hands of light
while tongues and muscles blood and song
danced outside of memory
feet weightless on a pagan shore.

Used by permission of Steelrail Music Inc. ℗1992 Socan.

Tarantella

For Leo Zarafino

I canzuni that you teach me
leave the trees you climb and cut
each summer morning
standing
as you turn your hands to song.

Let's talk for a moment.
Stop cutting those trees in Rosedale
stop and drink your espresso
here beside me
and sing of the spider dance.

The tarantella howls out of you.
Not like the costumes
i mangia checchi have grown used to.
I know you need your hands to climb
and cut and pass the tree limbs down
but stop here
with that song
rough as a dusted sandal on dry earth
long as a night of bonfires
lit in a village square.

U Canada   Canada
is colder than the thirty years
you've lived here.

If it does not need your song
it hasn't heard it yet.
You and the crows stuck in your throat
and the blisters
fighting the steel strings of guitars
you with the spider's song
twisting high above the trees
like a bird not meant to prey
like a Catholic
finally off his knees.

The Portuguese on College Street

Mikey, the wrestler doesn't see the change
doesn't see it any more
than he saw wrestling as a show
so he calls the sport a fake
claims Italians own the street
and crooks ruined his career.

But the Portuguese don't wrestle. Beat
the shit out of each other over parking
but they don't wrestle. They
roast their fish in their backyards
play accordions   mandolins
soccer on their Sundays.

At least the older guys do.
Guys my age and younger jam
down the pedals of Trans-Ams
bop and scratch their crotches
out of work and full of heat.

Mikey,
this was us
in the fifties   in the sixties
walking like peacocks
greeting the most recently sponsored cousin
telling this country to fuck off
'cause the heat from Calabria
was still in us.

Now we got towers and builders, Mikey.
Not just guys sweating and dying in falls
but owners, Mikey,
big company guys
and teachers   lawyers   doctors
not just
seamstresses and tailors.

And your cocaine, Mikey.
Who needs it?
The whole street on a winter day.
Nobody with a song on a summer day.

I want you to take my hand.
I want you to walk up
to the guy with the lunch bag and muscles
opening his arms to greet his running kid
stepping on to the porch and eased by
the scent of roasted sardines,
and shake his hand.
He's us back then, Mike.

Wish him well
don't wrestle him or he'll
kick you to the street
his hunger has reason
no habit
and a clear sight on the future
something like we used to know.

The Song Is a Poem

For Louis Perez and Los Lobos

La la lalala la Bamba –
as Ritchie Valens turned the phrase
from a bordello south of the border
to your rendering

and a poem
born from the barrio
a corrido bred from the Revolution
wails across mountains
and into the automobiles
of America
Canada
and the rest of the English
speaking world.

That Valens was Valenzuela
is okay to say now.

That songs in two minutes
do what a poem fights a lifetime to do
is unintentional

but we have books
where a voice used to be
communication
where the heart or soul should sing.

And when my poet friends
ask
what is the difference
between a poem and a song

I answer
many things

but nothing satisfies me
as much
as the language
sailing off the page
book readers
and singers
well-versed and dancing
in a sea of poems and songs.

Cantatore

Oral
poetry is like an unwhispered
word

in a country
where children
run
home across fields
play by a river
and climb for the
fruit
of the tallest of trees.

Oral poetry
is a song after
death
in an un-nourished village
caked in the sun
with armies rumbling through.

Oral poetry
is a dance of two
lovers
in the high grass of meadows

and the singer
at a well or a fountain
leaving his heart
for a cool cup of water.

Columbus

When news and history meet
and this melding sweeps the sky
brilliant with a head of fire
the random faces of vain centuries
cease their masquerade.

Tired ships
sail a cloudless eye beneath the moon.

Flags resting below deck
dream of drowning horses.

At the edge of the world
abandoned men watch as though in Purgatory's hold.

Watch for Heaven and beyond see Paradise.
There are no circles of wisdom and experience.

The natural dream has ended.
Fear locks the light which cracks the mind.

On a sanded beach wild dogs surround
the chest of the moon as it billows to the shore.

When memory sweeps the sky
a head of fire
hands the world to dogs.

The ships come and go
through waters reflecting cross and mast.

Behind is left false gold
and the scent of spice and unknown hands.

More ships arrive
and contours are etched into the deep face of the sea.

This   in the days that last five hundred years.
This
in time before and time to come. This
before and after time.
This   resisting the fangs of wild dogs.
This
closing staircase door both top and bottom.
This   leaving dead. This   sailing
home and back and home and back again. This
to round the world's sharp edges.
To save those hanging at its edge.
This   to forget the bursting lungs of horses.

This   to seal the crack upon the skull.
This   to free eyes from the moon.

This   for gold and reason.

Brilliant with a head of fire
five hundred years turns dream to nightmare.

Five hundred years
and the dawn does not know the quiet night.
Five hundred years
and the tree does not know its seed.
Five hundred years
and the water turns again to stone.
Five hundred years
and flags stand at their beginning.
Five hundred years
and Heaven fears its masquerade.

And at the edge of the sea
Paradise
holds an ape
that in turn holds a flower
as a tail of light
rises in the corner of its eye.

Tarantella II

I sing for you a tarantella
now
a tarantella for your feet

squeezed into a room of women
with bodies hard as steel
men filled with wines and fruit.

I give to you this tarantella
as it is meant to give
not listen to
against the wall of reason

folding its arms comfortably in the
ears of a lonely century.

This tarantella
with the eyes of a child
fighting his sister at the end
of a birthday table for gifts

lifts off the floor of a shack
in a country calling sun.

This tarantella
does not turn its face from you
but wants you to live on
like your mother at your birth.

This tarantella does not
forget its name at Ellis Island or Halifax Harbour
but lives in the hands of field workers
who pass it on to bricklayers
women working in factories
men paving roads
and their children.

And if you hear it
dance
and if you see it
sing
for it is for you it comes 'round
twisting inside itself
sweating across a wooden floor
taking your hand.

College Street

Scorsese doesn't come here. Did
you know
you can go back of San Francesco's Church
and women with the strength of mules
will take their aging husbands'
arms and dance an afternoon away.

Did you know Columbus didn't make it.
Didn't
find the pleasure these women know
and their pain
men dead on faulty bridges   unsafe
skyscrapers   sons
doped up speakers blasting
through Camaros.

Nobody talks of Sacco and Vanzetti
here. Oh sure
once in a while the shoemaker
down on Clinton Street brings
up Marconi   one of those great Americans
but his walls are pasted
with pin-up girls from the daily paper.

And at the *Gatto Nero* one old man
came in during the last World Cup
cursing us all for sitting around a T.V.
'cause as he put it, 'When I was young
I used my legs to walk. If it was
up to me I'd break all your legs
like Mussolini!'

Something remains. But the women
age
and their sons and daughters
live in suburbs   Woodbridge
Vaughn   Oak Ridges
drive in on Saints' Days
and wonder what all their parents'
struggle was about.

'The old Italians are dying' –
like Ferlingetti said but he
said that at least ten years ago
and they're still here. Dying

is as long as it takes for a son to
love or hate his father
a daughter to curse or accept her mother's
superstitious ways. Maybe that's

why most of my friends marry
or chase down blondes. Men or women
it's as if long golden curls
were a passport to a country
you could avoid bringing the baggage
of old world suffering to.

We carry heritage a long way here.
Bellhops to a dying culture
you might say dwelling in history
because we have stopped living.

Tonight I'll walk the neighbourhood
or just a little past   to the café
by the moviehouse
and listen to Domenico

talk again about the Ethiopians
and Somalians   and the
ever present Portuguese and I'll
hear him out,
'Yeah, sure, ten cigarettes and one
coffee. How can I run a café?

Did ya come to see *Raging Bull*?'

'No,' I tell him. 'I came out
because there's something in your eyes,
your way of speaking,
I thought I recognized.'

And when he tells me that I think
too much and that poems
are nice but hey there's no money
I tell him that he's probably right
and return home
where there's nothing lost or found
and stop off for a Coke and chat
at the Korean's.

And tomorrow
though my boots need no repair
I'll go out to the shoemaker's
understand why he's never fixed his radio
and wait with him for Marconi.

Canadian Broadcasting Corporation

On the road to Ottawa
Tom does Roger Daltrey and Dylan
impersonations. His 'I can see for miles...'
and 'Oh, I didn't know that...' are perfect.

In the studio later
promoting the show I'm to give
the interviewer says,
'Okay, so, Joseph Maviglia. Hm,
you've worked eighteen years in construction
and write songs. What's one
got to do with the other? I
expected you to show up with a hardhat.'

'No, it's not that way. You see
you have
Stan Rogers singing about fishermen,
Lightfoot sang about the railroad
and Rita MacNeil, she doesn't bring
a bag of coal on stage before she
starts to sing, does she? Does Stan Rogers,
I know he's dead, but, did he bring
out a fishing rod and start casting
before he sang his songs?'

The interviewer is watching me.

'These songs are about
the men that built the road
you drove to work on, the buildings
around you, the table you're sitting
at, the sidewalks you walk. These

songs are about two, three
generations of workers from Southern Italy.'

'Hm, I didn't know that.'

'These songs are about
the songs
that have not been sung
the songs
that you'll come to know
like a thing finally at home
a home
like a song
with a tree
at the edge of an entrance

where a boat filled with strangers
leaves no one
behind and forgetting
ahead only
of the boat behind it
the boat
filled with silence
rounding the sea
which has always been round
though to you
this I'm sure must sound new.'

In this Fiction

In this fiction where the eye
is trained
is no more an immigrant's lament
no longer a citizen's comfort
no hand is offered
no offering of a hand
would make a difference.

This is because
at the end of the day
no matter what day it is
there are those who go home tired
and those who don't go home at all.

And if I am asked
by you
by anyone
what the value of perception
is
I never
find an answer
but I know
this is a fiction

you
and I
the lament
the eye   and the comfort
trying hard to be
what the space between two hands is not.

Man Pulling a Star from His Throat: Poem for a Refugee

He pulls the moon down through a jug of wine.
The twentieth century
now at his feet
he opens his palms
and shows the scars of labour
the blood of his heart
his empty hands
never holding anything for long.

All you need to hate for
he can be. His language
loud that makes you hot
then wet. His laughter
and accordions that fill your
festivals. His screams
and his boorish wife
and obese children
who never eat in the same restaurants
as you.

He pulls a star out of his throat.
This is the last man
falling to his knees
in front of a patch of garden
shaded by skyscrapers
and maple trees.

But listen. His children
and his wife are not with him
in this alley you have walked to.

His eyes
laugh without echo
and you
the fortunate
observer
perfect
and alone

see nothing but the sun's descent.
And death
though it seems late in arriving
may be recognized by day's end
so that sleep
comes soundly
and leaves without a trace.

But the dog in the next yard
slurps up the last drops of wine left by the jug.
And in the lining of the soul
where it is hard to see
a hand
reaches and touches a fingertip
and the howl of a woman is never complete.

You turn to this sound
so don't tell me
you understand good food
and can ignore the tired city moon
and walk on
but don't see this man
vomiting
dropping his hands to his thighs
wishing at first
your eyes were a long jug of wine
but needing you to hold him
and tell him
he is no longer on the water.

Notes

P. 14. The use of *American* in 'Carlo's Dream' and 'There Is a Country' is used to represent North America. The term was and is still used by many who immigrated from Southern Europe to refer to *both* Canada and the United States.

P. 31. 'Brancaleone' is a small fishing and tourist town on the Ionian coast of Calabria. It is the town that Cesare Pavese was detained in by Fascists.

P. 33. Reggio di Calabria is the capital of Calabria. *Reggitani* are the inhabitants of the area.

P. 38. Salvatore Giuliano was an twentieth-century brigand who worked to liberate Sicilians from the Mafia on the western half of the island.

P. 49. 'Poetry makes nothing happen' is from W.H. Auden's 'In Memory of W.B. Yeats.'

P. 59. Geremio is the protagonist's father in Pietro di Donato's 1939 novel *Christ in Concrete.*

P. 66. Walter Rodney was Guyanese leader assassinated in 1980.

P. 87. Lyrics in 'On Winning a Juno Award' are from *Father, It's Time* used by permission of Steelrail Music P 1991 © Joseph Maviglia, SOCAN.

P. 92. *I mangia cheechi* translates roughly as cake eaters, a slang put down used by Southern Italians referring to anyone who does not share Italian heritage or abandons it for North American ways.

P.105. Sacco and Vanzetti were American industrial workers of Italian descent accused of murder and executed in Boston in 1927.

P.106. 'The old Italians are dying' is from the San Franciscan poet Lawrence Ferlinghetti's 'The Old Italians Dying.'

Acknowledgements

Some of these poems have been published in earlier versions in the following magazines and journals: *The Apostle's Bar, Arc, The Canadian Forum, Cross-Canada Writers' Quarterly, The Dalhousie Review, The eyetalian, The Fiddlehead, Freefall, The Greenfield Review, The Little Magazine, Labour / Le Travail, Paperwork: An Anthology of Work Poetry, Vice Versa* and *Voices in Italian Americana.*

Some of these poems have also been featured on CBC Radio FM (*Cloud 9* with Ricardo Keenes-Douglas), CHIN Radio with Lorenzo Vallecchi, CIUT FM (*Invoking the Muse* with Matthew Remski), CKCU FM (Carleton University, Ottawa), CBLT TV (Toronto), CFMT Channel 47 with Dino Cavaluzzo, CITY TV (Toronto) and TV Ontario's Workweek.

Also, thanks to Hratch Arabian, Austin Clarke, Mary di Michele, D.G. Jones, Mr Layton, Richard Lemm, Christopher Levenson, Mr Mitchell, Antonino Mazza, Tony Nardi, Alfredo Romano, Cameron Smith, Tom Wayman and Dale Zeiroth, and the organizers of the many readings ans conferences I've performed at. And most of all, thanks to Judith Ramirez for her love and support.

The author would like to thank The Ontario Arts Council, The Toronto Arts Council and The Ministry of Multiculturalism and Citizenship for their support during the creation of this work.

J.M.